The Top Football Club Quiz Book 2017

By David Jones

Introduction

This is a short-based unofficial quiz book based on the 49 clubs that have played within the Premier League since it started in 1992.

The League is made up of 20 teams each playing 38 matches each (playing each other twice, home and away) totalling 380 matches in a season.

Since the inception of the league in 1992, only six clubs have won the title: -

Manchester United (13)
Chelsea (5)
Arsenal (3)
Manchester City (2)
Blackburn Rovers (1)
Leicester City (1)

The questions range from easy to hard and are broken down by club.

Hope you enjoy.

The teams that have played in the Premier League since it began in 1992 up to 2017 - 2018 season are as follows: -

AFC BOURNEMOUTH
ARSENAL FC
ASTON VILLA FC
BARNSLEY FC
BIRMINGHAM CITY FC
BLACKBURN ROVERS FC
BLACKPOOL FC
BOLTON WANDERERS FC
BRADFORD CITY AFC
BRIGHTON & HOVE ALBION FC
BURNLEY FC
CARDIFF CITY FC
CHARLTON ATHLETIC AFC
CHELSEA FC
COVENTRY CITY FC
CRYSTAL PALACE
DERBY COUNTY FC
EVERTON FC
FULHAM FC
HUDDERSFIELD TOWN AFC
HULL CITY AFC
IPSWICH TOWN FC
LEEDS UNITED FC
LEICESTER CITY FC
LIVERPOOL FC
MANCHESTER CITY FC
MANCHESTER UTD FC
MIDDLESBOROUGH FC

NEWCASTLE UNITED FC
NORWICH CITY FC
NOTTINGHAM FOREST FC
OLDHAM ATHLETIC FC
PORTSMOUTH FC
QUEENS PARK RANGERS FC
READING FC
SHEFFIELD UNITED FC
SHEFFIELD WEDNESDAY FC
SOUTHAMPTON FC
STOKE CITY FC
SUNDERLAND AFC
SWANSEA CITY AFC
SWINDON TOWN FC
TOTTENHAM HOTSPUR FC
WATFORD FC
WEST BROMWICH ALBION FC
WEST HAM UNITED FC
WIGAN ATHLETIC FC
WIMBLEDON FC
WOLVERHAMPTON WANDERERS FC

AFC Bournemouth

1. What year were Bournemouth founded?

2. What was the original name of the team that was founded?

3. What ground did they play at first?

4. Who was the first kit manufacturer?

5. Who were the first kit sponsors?

6. Who was the first manager / Secretary?

7. Who is the current 2017/18 Manager?

8. Who is the current 2017/18 Club Captain?

9. Which player has made the most appearances for the club as of 2017?

10. Who is the all-time top goal scorer as of 2017?

11. As at 2017 who currently holds the record for most goals scored in a season?

12. What is the name of the current ground?

Arsenal FC

1. What year were Arsenal founded?

2. What was the original name of the team that was founded?

3. What ground did they play at first?

4. Who was the first kit manufacturer?

5. Who were the first kit sponsors?

6. Who was the first manager / Secretary?

7. Who is the current 2017/18 Manager?

8. Who is the current 2017/18 Club Captain?

9. Which player has made the most appearances for the club as of 2017?

10. Who is the all-time top goal scorer as of 2017?

11. As of 2017 how many times have they won the FA cup?

12. As at 2017 who currently holds the record for most goals scored in a season?

13. What is the name of the current ground?

14. When was the ladies team officially founded?

15. Where do the Ladies play their home games?

16. Who is the current 2017 manager of the ladies' team?

Aston Villa FC

1. What year were Aston Villa founded?
2. Who is the clubs main rival?
3. What ground did they play at first?
4. Who was the first kit manufacturer?
5. Who were the first kit sponsors?
6. Who was the first manager / Secretary?
7. Who is the current 2017/18 Manager?
8. Who is the current 2017/18 Club Captain?
9. Which player has made the most appearances for the club as of 2017?
10. Who is the all-time top goal scorer as of 2017?
11. As of 2017 how many times have they won the FA cup?
12. As at 2017 who currently holds the record for most goals scored in a season?
13. What is the name of the current ground?
14. When was the ladies team officially founded?

15. Where do the Ladies play their home games?

16. Who is the current 2017 manager of the ladies' team?

Barnsley FC

1. What year were Barnsley founded?
2. What was the original name of the team that was founded?
3. What ground did they play at first?
4. Who was the first kit manufacturer?
5. Who were the first kit sponsors?
6. Who was the first manager / Secretary?
7. Who is the current 2017/18 Manager?
8. Who is the current 2017/18 Club Captain?
9. Which player has made the most appearances for the club as of 2017?
10. Who is the all-time top goal scorer as of 2017?
11. As of 2017 how many times have they won the FA cup?
12. As at 2017 who currently holds the record for most goals scored in a season?
13. What is the name of the current ground?

14. When was the ladies team officially founded?

15. Where do the ladies play their home games?

16. Who is the current 2017 manager of the ladies' team?

Birmingham City FC

1. What year were Birmingham founded?
2. What was the original name of the team that was founded?
3. What ground did they play at first?
4. Who was the first kit manufacturer?
5. Who were the first kit sponsors?
6. Who was the first manager / Secretary?
7. Who is the current 2017/18 Manager?
8. Who is the current 2017/18 Club Captain?
9. Which player has made the most appearances for the club as of 2017?
10. Who is the all-time top goal scorer as of 2017?
11. As of 2017 how many times have they been runners up in the FA cup?
12. As at 2017 who currently holds the record for most goals scored in a season?
13. What is the name of the current ground?

14. When was the ladies team officially founded?

15. Where do the ladies play their home games?

16. Who is the current 2017 manager of the ladies' team?

Blackburn Rovers FC

1. What year were Blackburn founded?
2. What ground did they play at first?
3. Who was the first kit manufacturer?
4. Who were the first kit sponsors?
5. Who was the first manager / Secretary?
6. Who is the current 2017/18 Manager?
7. Who is the current 2017/18 Club Captain?
8. Which player has made the most appearances for the club as of 2017?
9. Who is the all-time top goal scorer as of 2017?
10. As of 2017 how many times have they won the FA cup?
11. As at 2017 who currently holds the record for most goals scored in a season?
12. What is the name of the current ground?
13. When was the ladies team officially founded?

14. Where do the Ladies play their home games?

15. Who is the current 2017 manager of the ladies' team?

Blackpool FC

1. What year were Blackpool founded?
2. Who is the clubs main rival?
3. What ground did they play at first?
4. Who was the first kit manufacturer?
5. Who were the first kit sponsors?
6. Who was the first manager / Secretary?
7. Who is the current 2017/18 Manager?
8. Who is the current 2017/18 Club Captain?
9. Which player has made the most appearances for the club as of 2017?
10. Who is the all-time top goal scorer as of 2017?
11. As of 2017 how many times have they won the FA cup?
12. As at 2017 who currently holds the record for most goals scored in a season?
13. What is the name of the current ground?
14. When was the ladies team officially founded?

15. Where do the Ladies play their home games?

16. Who is the current 2017 manager of the ladies' team?

Bolton Wanderers FC

1. What year were Bolton founded?
2. What was the original name of the team that was founded?
3. What ground did they play at first?
4. Who was the first kit manufacturer?
5. Who were the first kit sponsors?
6. Who was the first manager / Secretary?
7. Who is the current 2017/18 Manager?
8. Who is the current 2017/18 Club Captain?
9. Which player has made the most appearances for the club as of 2017?
10. Who is the all-time top goal scorer as of 2017?
11. As of 2017 how many times have they won the FA cup?
12. As at 2017 who currently holds the record for most goals scored in a season?
13. What is the name of the current ground?

Bradford City AFC

1. What year were Bradford founded?
2. Who is the clubs main rival?
3. What ground did they play at first?
4. Who was the first kit manufacturer?
5. Who were the first kit sponsors?
6. Who was the first manager / Secretary?
7. Who is the current 2017/18 Manager?
8. Who is the current 2017/18 Club Captain?
9. Which player has made the most appearances for the club as of 2017?
10. Who is the all-time top goal scorer as of 2017?
11. As of 2017 how many times have they won the FA cup?
12. As at 2017 who currently holds the record for most goals scored in a season?
13. What is the name of the current ground?
14. When was the ladies team officially founded?

15. Where do the Ladies play their home games?

16. Who is the current 2017 manager of the ladies' team?

Brighton & Hove Albion FC

1. What year were Brighton founded?
2. Who is the clubs main rival?
3. What ground did they play at first?
4. Who was the first kit manufacturer?
5. Who were the first kit sponsors?
6. Who was the first manager / Secretary?
7. Who is the current 2017/18 Manager?
8. Who is the current 2017/18 Club Captain?
9. Which player has made the most appearances for the club as of 2017?
10. Who is the all-time top goal scorer as of 2017?
11. As of 2017 how many times have they been runners up in the FA cup?
12. As at 2017 who currently holds the record for most goals scored in a season?
13. What is the name of the current ground?
14. When was the ladies team officially founded?

15. Where do the Ladies play their home games?

16. Who is the current 2017 manager of the ladies' team?

Burnley FC

1. What year were Burnley founded?
2. What was the original name of the team that was founded?
3. What ground did they play at first?
4. Who was the first kit manufacturer?
5. Who were the first kit sponsors?
6. Who was the first manager / Secretary?
7. Who is the current 2017/18 Manager?
8. Who is the current 2017/18 Club Captain?
9. Which player has made the most appearances for the club as of 2017?
10. Who is the all-time top goal scorer as of 2017?
11. As of 2017 how many times have they won the FA cup?
12. As at 2017 who currently holds the record for most goals scored in a season?
13. What is name of current ground?

14. When was the ladies team officially founded?

15. Where do the Ladies play their home games?

16. Who is the current 2017 manager of the ladies' team?

Cardiff City FC

1. What year were Cardiff founded?
2. What was the original name of the team that was founded?
3. What ground did they play at first?
4. Who was the first kit manufacturer?
5. Who were the first kit sponsors?
6. Who was the first manager / Secretary?
7. Who is the current 2017/18 Manager?
8. Who is the current 2017/18 Club Captain?
9. Which player has made the most appearances for the club as of 2017?
10. Who is the all-time top goal scorer as of 2017?
11. As of 2017 how many times have they won the FA cup?
12. As at 2017 who currently holds the record for most goals scored in a season?
13. What is the name of the current ground?

14. When was the ladies team officially founded?

15. Where do the Ladies play their home games?

16. Who is the current 2017 manager of the ladies' team?

Charlton Athletic AFC

1. What year were Charlton founded?
2. Who is the clubs main rival?
3. What ground did they play at first?
4. Who was the first kit manufacturer?
5. Who were the first kit sponsors?
6. Who was the first manager / Secretary?
7. Who is the current 2017/18 Manager?
8. Who is the current 2017/18 Club Captain?
9. Which player has made the most appearances for the club as of 2017?
10. Who is the all-time top goal scorer as of 2017?
11. As of 2017 how many times have they won the FA cup?
12. As at 2017 who currently holds the record for most goals scored in a season?
13. What is the name of the current ground?

14. When were the ladies team officially founded?

15. Where do the Ladies play their home games?

16. Who is the current 2017 manager of the ladies' team?

Chelsea FC

1. What year were Chelsea founded?
2. Who is the clubs main rival?
3. What ground did they play at first?
4. Who was the first kit manufacturer?
5. Who were the first kit sponsors?
6. Who was the first manager / Secretary?
7. Who is the current 2017/18 Manager?
8. Who is the current 2017/18 Club Captain?
9. Which player has made the most appearances for the club as of 2017?
10. Who is the all-time top goal scorer as of 2017?
11. As of 2017 how many times have they won the FA cup?
12. As at 2017 who currently holds the record for most goals scored in a season?
13. What is the name of the current ground?
14. When was the ladies team officially founded?

15. Where do the Ladies play their home games?

16. Who is the current 2017 manager of the ladies' team?

Coventry City FC

1. What year were Coventry founded?
2. What was the original name of the team that was founded?
3. What ground did they play at first?
4. Who was the first kit manufacturer?
5. Who were the first kit sponsors?
6. Who was the first manager / Secretary?
7. Who is the current 2017/18 Manager?
8. Who is the current 2017/18 Club Captain?
9. Which player has made the most appearances for the club as of 2017?
10. Who is the all-time top goal scorer as of 2017?
11. As of 2017 how many times have they won the FA cup?
12. As at 2017 who currently holds the record for most goals scored in a season?
13. What is the name of the current ground?

14. When was the ladies team officially founded?

15. Where do the Ladies play their home games?

16. Who is the current 2017 manager of the ladies' team?

Crystal Palace FC

1. What year were Crystal Palace founded?
2. Who is the clubs main rival?
3. What ground did they play at first?
4. Who was the first kit manufacturer?
5. Who were the first kit sponsors?
6. Who was the first manager / Secretary?
7. Who is the current 2017/18 Manager?
8. Who is the current 2017/18 Club Captain?
9. Which player has made the most appearances for the club as of 2017?
10. Who is the all-time top goal scorer as of 2017?
11. As of 2017 how many times have they been runners up in the FA cup?
12. As at 2017 who currently holds the record for most goals scored in a season?
13. What is the name of the current ground?
14. When was the ladies team officially founded?

15. Where do the Ladies play their home games?

16. Who is the current 2017 manager of the ladies' team?

Derby County FC

1. What year were Derby founded?
2. Who is the clubs main rival?
3. What ground did they play at first?
4. Who was the first kit manufacturer?
5. Who were the first kit sponsors?
6. Who was the first manager / Secretary?
7. Who is the current 2017/18 Manager?
8. Who is the current 2017/18 Club Captain?
9. Which player has made the most appearances for the club as of 2017?
10. Who is the all-time top goal scorer as of 2017?
11. As of 2017 how many times have they won the FA cup?
12. As at 2017 who currently holds the record for most goals scored in a season?
13. What is the name of the current ground?
14. When was the ladies team officially founded?

15. Where do the Ladies play their home games?

16. Who is the current 2017 manager of the ladies' team?

Everton FC

1. What year were Everton founded?

2. What was the original name of the team that was founded?

3. What ground did they play at first?

4. Who was the first kit manufacturer?

5. Who were the first kit sponsors?

6. Who was the first manager / Secretary?

7. Who is the current 2017/18 Manager?

8. Who is the current 2017/18 Club Captain?

9. Which player has made the most appearances for the club as of 2017?

10. Who is the all-time top goal scorer as of 2017?

11. As of 2017 how many times have they won the FA cup?

12. As at 2017 who currently holds the record for most goals scored in a season?

13. What is the name of the current ground?

14. When was the ladies team officially founded?

15. Where do the Ladies play their home games?

16. Who is the current 2017 manager of the ladies' team?

Fulham FC

1. What year were Fulham founded?

2. What was the original name of the team that was founded?

3. What ground did they play at first?

4. Who was the first kit manufacturer?

5. Who were the first kit sponsors?

6. Who was the first manager / Secretary?

7. Who is the current 2017/18 Manager?

8. Who is the current 2017/18 Club Captain?

9. Which player has made the most appearances for the club as of 2017?

10. Who is the all-time top goal scorer as of 2017?

11. As of 2017 how many times have they been runners up in the FA cup?

12. As at 2017 who currently holds the record for most goals scored in a season?

13. What is the name of the current ground?

14. When was the ladies team officially founded?

15. Where did the Ladies play their home games?

16. What year did the team Dissolve?

Huddersfield Town AFC

1. What year were Huddersfield founded?
2. Who is the clubs main rival?
3. What ground did they play at first?
4. Who was the first kit manufacturer?
5. Who were the first kit sponsors?
6. Who was the first manager / Secretary?
7. Who is the Manager in 2017-18 season?
8. Who is the 2017 Club Captain?
9. Which player has made most appearances?
10. Who is the all-time top goal scorer as of 2017?
11. Who many times have they won the FA cup?
12. Who was highest league scorer in one season?
13. What is name of current ground?
14. When was the ladies team officially founded?

15. Where do the Ladies play their home games?

16. Who is the current 2017 manager of the ladies' team?

Hull City AFC

1. What year were Hull founded?
2. Who is the clubs main rival?
3. What ground did they play at first?
4. Who was the first kit manufacturer?
5. Who were the first kit sponsors?
6. Who was the first manager / Secretary?
7. Who is the current 2017/18 Manager?
8. Who is the current 2017/18 Club Captain?
9. Which player has made the most appearances for the club as of 2017?
10. Who is the all-time top goal scorer as of 2017?
11. As of 2017 how many times have they been runners up in the FA cup?
12. As at 2017 who currently holds the record for most goals scored in a season?
13. What is name of current ground?

14. When were the ladies team officially founded?

15. Where do the Ladies play their home games?

16. Who is the current 2017 manager of the ladies' team?

Ipswich Town FC

1. What year were Ipswich founded?
2. Who is the clubs main rival?
3. What ground did they play at first?
4. Who was the first manager / Secretary?
5. Who is the current 2017/18 Manager?
6. Who is the current 2017/18 Club Captain?
7. Which player has made the most appearances for the club as of 2017?
8. Who is the all-time top goal scorer as of 2017?
9. As of 2017 how many times have they won the FA cup?
10. As at 2017 who currently holds the record for most goals scored in a season?
11. What is the name of the current ground?
12. Where do the Ladies play their home games?
13. Who is the current 2017 manager of the ladies' team?

Leeds United FC

1. What year were Leeds founded?
2. Who is the clubs main rival?
3. What ground did they play at first?
4. Who was the first kit manufacturer?
5. Who were the first kit sponsors?
6. Who was the first manager / Secretary?
7. Who is the current 2017/18 Manager?
8. Who is the current 2017/18 Club Captain?
9. Which player has made the most appearances for the club as of 2017?
10. Who is the all-time top goal scorer as of 2017?
11. As of 2017 how many times have they won the FA cup?
12. As at 2017 who currently holds the record for most goals scored in a season?
13. What is the name of the current ground?
14. When was the ladies team officially founded?

15. Where do the Ladies play their home games?

16. Who is the current 2017 manager of the ladies' team?

Leicester City FC

1. What year were Leicester founded?
2. What was the original name of the team that was founded?
3. What ground did they play at first?
4. Who was the first kit manufacturer?
5. Who were the first kit sponsors?
6. Who was the first manager / Secretary?
7. Who is the current 2017/18 Manager?
8. Who is the current 2017/18 Club Captain?
9. Which player has made the most appearances for the club as of 2017?
10. Who is the all-time top goal scorer as of 2017?
11. As of 2017 how many times have they been runners up in the FA cup?
12. As at 2017 who currently holds the record for most goals scored in a season?
13. What is the name of the current ground

14. When was the ladies team officially founded?

15. Where do the Ladies play their home games?

16. Who is the current 2017 manager of the ladies' team?

Liverpool FC

1. What year were Liverpool founded?
2. Who is the clubs main rival?
3. What ground did they play at first?
4. Who was the first kit manufacturer?
5. Who were the first kit sponsors?
6. Who was the first manager / Secretary?
7. Who is the current 2017/18 Manager?
8. Who is the current 2017/18 Club Captain?
9. Which player has made the most appearances for the club as of 2017?
10. Who is the all-time top goal scorer as of 2017?
11. As of 2017 how many times have they won the FA cup?
12. As at 2017 who currently holds the record for most goals scored in a season?
13. What is the name of the current ground?
14. When was the ladies team officially founded?

15. Where do the Ladies play their home games?

16. Who is the current 2017 manager of the ladies' team?

Manchester City FC

1. What year were Manchester City founded?
2. What was the original name of the team that was founded?
3. What ground did they play at first?
4. Who was the first kit manufacturer?
5. Who were the first kit sponsors?
6. Who was the first manager / Secretary?
7. Who is the current 2017/18 Manager?
8. Who is the current 2017/18 Club Captain?
9. Which player has made the most appearances for the club as of 2017?
10. Who is the all-time top goal scorer as of 2017?
11. As of 2017 how many times have they won the FA cup?
12. As at 2017 who currently holds the record for most goals scored in a season?
13. What is the name of the current ground?

14. When was the ladies team officially founded?

15. Where do the Ladies play their home games?

16. Who is the current 2017 manager of the ladies' team?

Manchester United FC

1. What year were Manchester United founded?
2. What was the original name of the team that was founded?
3. What ground did they play at first?
4. Who was the first kit manufacturer?
5. Who were the first kit sponsors?
6. Who was the first manager / Secretary?
7. Who is the current 2017/18 Manager?
8. Who is the current 2017/18 Club Captain?
9. Which player has made the most appearances for the club as of 2017?
10. Who is the all-time top goal scorer as of 2017?
11. As of 2017 how many times have they won the FA cup?
12. As at 2017 who currently holds the record for most goals scored in a season?
13. What is the name of the current ground?

Middlesborough FC

1. What year were Middlesborough founded?
2. Who is the clubs main rival?
3. What ground did they play at first?
4. Who was the first kit manufacturer?
5. Who were the first kit sponsors?
6. Who was the first manager / Secretary?
7. Who is the current 2017/18 Manager?
8. Who is the current 2017/18 Club Captain?
9. Which player has made the most appearances for the club as of 2017?
10. Who is the all-time top goal scorer as of 2017?
11. As of 2017 how many times have they been runners-up in the FA cup?
12. As at 2017 who currently holds the record for most goals scored in a season?
13. What is the name of the current ground?
14. When was the ladies team officially founded?

15. Where do the Ladies play their home games?

16. Who is the current 2017 manager of the ladies' team?

Newcastle United FC

1. What year were Newcastle founded?
2. Who is the clubs main rival?
3. What ground did they play at first?
4. Who was the first kit manufacturer?
5. Who were the first kit sponsors?
6. Who was the first manager / Secretary?
7. Who is the current 2017/18 Manager?
8. Who is the current 2017/18 Club Captain?
9. Which player has made the most appearances for the club as of 2017?
10. Who is the all-time top goal scorer as of 2017?
11. As of 2017 how many times have they won the FA cup?
12. As at 2017 who currently holds the record for most goals scored in a season?
13. What is the name of the current ground?
14. When was the ladies team officially founded?

15. Where do the ladies play their home games?

16. Who is the current 2017 manager of the ladies' team?

Norwich City FC

1. What year were Norwich founded?
2. Who is the clubs main rival?
3. What ground did they play at first?
4. Who was the first kit manufacturer?
5. Who were the first kit sponsors?
6. Who was the first manager / Secretary?
7. Who is the current 2017/18 Manager?
8. Who is the current 2017/18 Club Captain?
9. Which player has made the most appearances for the club as of 2017?
10. Who is the all-time top goal scorer as of 2017?
11. As at 2017 who currently holds the record for most goals scored in a season?
12. What is the name of the current ground?
13. When was the ladies team officially founded?
14. Where do the ladies play their home games?

15. Who is the current 2017 manager of the ladies' team?

Nottingham Forest FC

1. What year were Nottingham Forest founded?
2. Who is the clubs main rival?
3. What ground did they play at first?
4. Who was the first kit manufacturer?
5. Who were the first kit sponsors?
6. Who was the first manager / Secretary?
7. Who is the current 2017/18 Manager?
8. Who is the current 2017/18 Club Captain?
9. Which player has made the most appearances for the club as of 2017?
10. Who is the all-time top goal scorer as of 2017?
11. As of 2017 how many times have they won the FA cup?
12. As at 2017 who currently holds the record for most goals scored in a season?
13. What is the name of the current ground?
14. When was the ladies team officially founded?

15. Where do the ladies play their home games?

16. Who is the current 2017 manager of the ladies' team?

Oldham Athletic FC

1. What year were Oldham founded?
2. Who is the clubs main rival?
3. What ground did they play at first?
4. Who was the first kit manufacturer?
5. Who was the first manager / Secretary?
6. Who is the current 2017/18 Manager?
7. Who is the current 2017/18 Club Captain?
8. Which player has made the most appearances for the club as of 2017?
9. Who is the all-time top goal scorer as of 2017?
10. As of 2017 how many times have they been semi-finalists in the FA cup?
11. As at 2017 who currently holds the record for most goals scored in a season?
12. What is the name of the current ground?

Portsmouth FC

1. What year were Portsmouth founded?
2. Who is the clubs main rival?
3. What ground did they play at first?
4. Who was the first kit manufacturer?
5. Who were the first kit sponsors?
6. Who was the first manager / Secretary?
7. Who is the current 2017/18 Manager?
8. Who is the current 2017/18 Club Captain?
9. Which player has made the most appearances for the club as of 2017?
10. Who is the all-time top goal scorer as of 2017?
11. As of 2017 how many times have they won the FA cup?
12. As at 2017 who currently holds the record for most goals scored in a season?
13. What is name of current ground?
14. When was the ladies team officially founded?

15. Where do the Ladies play their home games?

16. Who is the current 2017 manager of the ladies' team?

Queens Park Rangers FC

1. What year were Queens Park founded?
2. What was the original name of the team that was founded?
3. What ground did they play at first?
4. Who was the first kit manufacturer?
5. Who were the first kit sponsors?
6. Who was the first manager / Secretary?
7. Who is the current 2017/18 Manager?
8. Who is the current 2017/18 Club Captain?
9. Which player has made the most appearances for the club as of 2017?
10. Who is the all-time top goal scorer as of 2017?
11. As of 2017 how many times have they been runners-up in the FA cup?
12. As at 2017 who currently holds the record for most goals scored in a season?
13. What is the name of the current ground?

14. When was the ladies team officially founded?

15. Where do the Ladies play their home games?

16. Who is the current 2017 manager of the ladies' team?

Reading FC

1. What year were Reading founded?
2. Who is the clubs main rival?
3. What ground did they play at first?
4. Who was the first kit manufacturer?
5. Who were the first kit sponsors?
6. Who was the first manager / Secretary?
7. Who is the current 2017/18 Manager?
8. Who is the current 2017/18 Club Captain?
9. Which player has made the most appearances for the club as of 2017?
10. Who is the all-time top goal scorer as of 2017?
11. As of 2017 how many times have they been semi-finalists in the FA cup?
12. As at 2017 who currently holds the record for most goals scored in a season?
13. What is name of current ground?

14. When were the ladies team officially founded?

15. Where do the Ladies play their home games?

16. Who is the current 2017 manager of the ladies' team?

Sheffield United FC

1. What year were Sheffield United founded?
2. Who is the clubs main rival?
3. What ground did they play at first?
4. Who was the first kit manufacturer?
5. Who were the first kit sponsors?
6. Who was the first manager / Secretary?
7. Who is the current 2017/18 Manager?
8. Who is the current 2017/18 Club Captain?
9. Which player has made the most appearances for the club as of 2017?
10. Who is the all-time top goal scorer as of 2017?
11. As of 2017 how many times have they won the FA cup?
12. As at 2017 who currently holds the record for most goals scored in a season?
13. What is the name of the current ground?
14. When was the ladies team officially founded?

15. Where do the Ladies play their home games?

16. Who is the current 2017 manager of the ladies' team?

Sheffield Wednesday FC

1. What year were Sheffield founded?
2. Who is the clubs main rival?
3. What ground did they play at first?
4. Who was the first kit manufacturer?
5. Who was the first manager / Secretary?
6. Who is the current 2017/18 Manager?
7. Who is the current 2017/18 Club Captain?
8. Which player has made the most appearances for the club as of 2017?
9. Who is the all-time top goal scorer as of 2017?
10. As of 2017 how many times have they won the FA cup?
11. As at 2017 who currently holds the record for most goals scored in a season?
12. What is the name of the current ground?
13. When was the ladies team officially founded?
14. Where do the ladies play their home games?

15. Who is the current 2017 manager of the ladies' team?

Southampton FC

1. What year were Southampton founded?
2. What was the name of the club when formed?
3. What ground did they play at first?
4. Who was the first kit manufacturer?
5. Who were the first kit sponsors?
6. Who was the first manager / Secretary?
7. Who is the current 2017/18 Manager?
8. Who is the current 2017/18 Club Captain?
9. Which player has made the most appearances for the club as of 2017?
10. Who is the all-time top goal scorer as of 2017?
11. As of 2017 how many times have they won the FA cup?
12. As at 2017 who currently holds the record for most goals scored in a season?
13. What is the name of the current ground?

14. When was the ladies team officially founded?

15. Where do the ladies play their home games?

16. Who is the current 2017 manager of the ladies' team?

Stoke City FC

1. What year were Stoke founded?
2. What was the original name of the team that was founded?
3. What ground did they play at first?
4. Who was the first kit manufacturer?
5. Who were the first kit sponsors?
6. Who was the first manager / Secretary?
7. Who is the current 2017/18 Manager?
8. Who is the current 2017/18 Club Captain?
9. Which player has made the most appearances for the club as of 2017?
10. Who is the all-time top goal scorer as of 2017?
11. As of 2017 how many times have they been runners up in the FA cup?
12. As at 2017 who currently holds the record for most goals scored in a season?
13. What is the name of the current ground?

14. When was the ladies team officially founded?

15. Where do the Ladies play their home games?

16. Who is the current 2017 manager of the ladies' team?

Sunderland AFC

1. What year were Sunderland founded?
2. What was the original name of the team that was founded?
3. What ground did they play at first?
4. Who was the first kit manufacturer?
5. Who were the first kit sponsors?
6. Who was the first manager / Secretary?
7. Who is the current 2017/18 Manager?
8. Who is the current 2017/18 Club Captain?
9. Which player has made the most appearances for the club as of 2017?
10. Who is the all-time top goal scorer as of 2017?
11. As of 2017 how many times have they won the FA cup?
12. As at 2017 who currently holds the record for most goals scored in a season?
13. What is the name of the current ground?

14. When was the ladies team officially founded?

15. Where do the Ladies play their home games?

16. Who is the current 2017 manager of the ladies' team?

Swansea City AFC

1. What year were Swansea founded?
2. What was the original name of the team that was founded?
3. What ground did they play at first?
4. Who was the first kit manufacturer?
5. Who were the first kit sponsors?
6. Who was the first manager / Secretary?
7. Who is the current 2017/18 Manager?
8. Who is the current 2017/18 Club Captain?
9. Which player has made the most appearances for the club as of 2017?
10. Who is the all-time top goal scorer as of 2017?
11. As of 2017 how many times have they been semi-finalists in the FA cup?
12. As at 2017 who currently holds the record for most goals scored in a season?
13. What is the name of the current ground?

14. When was the ladies team officially founded?

15. Where do the Ladies play their home games?

16. Who is the current 2017 manager of the ladies' team?

Swindon Town FC

1. What year were Swindon founded?
2. What was the original name of the team that was founded?
3. What ground did they play at first?
4. Who was the first kit manufacturer?
5. Who were the first kit sponsors?
6. Who was the first manager / Secretary?
7. Who is the current 2017/18 Manager?
8. Who is the current 2017/18 Club Captain?
9. Which player has made the most appearances for the club as of 2017?
10. Who is the all-time top goal scorer as of 2017?
11. As of 2017 how many times have they been semi-finalists in the FA cup?
12. As at 2017 who currently holds the record for most goals scored in a season?
13. What is the name of the current ground?

14. When was the ladies team officially founded?

15. Where do the ladies play their home games?

16. Who is the current 2017 manager of the ladies' team?

Tottenham Hotspur FC

1. What year were Tottenham founded?
2. What was the original name of the team that was founded?
3. What ground did they play at first?
4. Who was the first kit manufacturer?
5. Who were the first kit sponsors?
6. Who was the first manager / Secretary?
7. Who is the current 2017/18 Manager?
8. Who is the current 2017/18 Club Captain?
9. Which player has made the most appearances for the club as of 2017?
10. Who is the all-time top goal scorer as of 2017?
11. As of 2017 how many times have they won the FA cup?
12. As at 2017 who currently holds the record for most goals scored in a season?
13. What is the name of the current ground?

14. When was the ladies team officially founded?

15. Where do the Ladies play their home games?

16. Who is the current 2017 manager of the ladies' team?

Watford FC

1. What year were Watford founded?
2. What was the original name of the team that was founded?
3. What ground did they play at first?
4. Who was the first kit manufacturer?
5. Who were the first kit sponsors?
6. Who was the first manager / Secretary?
7. Who is the current 2017/18 Manager?
8. Who is the current 2017/18 Club Captain?
9. Which player has made the most appearances for the club as of 2017?
10. Who is the all-time top goal scorer as of 2017?
11. As of 2017 how many times have they been runners up in the FA cup?
12. As at 2017 who currently holds the record for most goals scored in a season?
13. What is name of current ground?

14. When was the ladies team officially founded?

15. Where do the Ladies play their home games?

16. Who is the current 2017 manager of the ladies' team?

West Bromwich Albion FC

1. What year were West Brom founded?
2. What was the original name of the team that was founded?
3. What ground did they play at first?
4. Who was the first kit manufacturer?
5. Who were the first kit sponsors?
6. Who was the first manager / Secretary?
7. Who is the current 2017/18 Manager?
8. Who is the current 2017/18 Club Captain?
9. Which player has made the most appearances for the club as of 2017?
10. Who is the all-time top goal scorer as of 2017?
11. As of 2017 how many times have they won the FA cup?
12. As at 2017 who currently holds the record for most goals scored in a season?
13. What is name of current ground?

14. When was the ladies team officially founded?

15. Where do the Ladies play their home games?

16. Who is the current 2017 manager of the ladies' team?

West Ham United FC

1. What year were West Ham founded?
2. What was the original name of the team that was founded?
3. What ground did they play at first?
4. Who was the first kit manufacturer?
5. Who were the first kit sponsors?
6. Who was the first manager / Secretary?
7. Who is the current 2017/18 Manager?
8. Who is the current 2017/18 Club Captain?
9. Which player has made the most appearances for the club as of 2017?
10. Who is the all-time top goal scorer as of 2017?
11. As of 2017 how many times have they won the FA cup?
12. As at 2017 who currently holds the record for most goals scored in a season?
13. What is name of current ground?

14. When was the ladies team officially founded?

15. Where do the ladies play their home games?

16. Who is the current 2017 manager of the ladies' team?

Wigan Athletic FC

1. What year were Wigan founded?
2. Who is the clubs main rival?
3. What ground did they play at first?
4. Who was the first kit manufacturer?
5. Who was the first manager / Secretary?
6. Who is the current 2017/18 Manager?
7. Who is the current 2017/18 Club Captain?
8. Which player has made the most appearances for the club as of 2017?
9. Who is the all-time top goal scorer as of 2017?
10. As of 2017 how many times have they won the FA cup?
11. As at 2017 who currently holds the record for most goals scored in a season?
12. What is name of current ground?

Wimbledon FC

1. What year were Wimbledon founded?
2. What was the original name of the team that was founded?
3. What ground did they play at first?
4. Who was the first kit manufacturer?
5. Who were the first kit sponsors?
6. Who was the first manager / Secretary?
7. Who is the Manager for Milton Keynes Dons in 2017-18 season?
8. Who is the 2017 Club Captain of Milton Keynes Dons?
9. Which player has made the most appearances for the club as of 2017?
10. Who is the all-time top goal scorer as of 2017?
11. As of 2017 how many times have they won the FA cup?
12. As at 2017 who currently holds the record for most goals scored in a season?

13. What is the name of MK dons current ground?

Wolverhampton Wanderers FC

1. What year were Wolves founded?
2. What was the original name of the team that was founded?
3. What ground did they play at first?
4. Who was the first kit manufacturer?
5. Who was the first manager / Secretary?
6. Who is the current 2017/18 Manager?
7. Who is the current 2017/18 Club Captain?
8. Which player has made the most appearances for the club as of 2017?
9. Who is the all-time top goal scorer as of 2017?
10. As of 2017 how many times have they won the FA cup?
11. As at 2017 who currently holds the record for most goals scored in a season?
12. What is the name of the current ground?
13. When was the ladies team officially founded?

14. Where do the Ladies play their home games?

15. Who is the current 2017 manager of the ladies' team?

Answers

AFC Bournemouth

1. 1899
2. Boscombe FC
3. Castlemain Avenue
4. Umbro
5. Reg Heynes Toyota
6. Vincent Kitcher
7. Eddie Howe
8. Simon Francis
9. Sean O'Driscoll (423)
10. Ron Eyre (202)
11. Ted MacDougall (42)
12. Dean Court

Arsenal FC

1. 1886
2. Royal Arsenal FC
3. Plumstead Common
4. Bukta

5. JVC
6. Thomas Mitchell
7. Arsene Wenger
8. Per Mertesacker
9. David O'Leary (722)
10. Thierry Henry (228)
11. 13
12. Ted Drake (44)
13. Emirates Stadium
14. 1987
15. Meadow Park
16. Pedro Martinez Losa

Aston Villa FC

1. 1874
2. Birmingham City
3. Aston Road
4. Umbro
5. Davenports
6. George Ramsay

7. Steve Bruce
8. John Terry
9. Charlie Aitken (657)
10. Billy Walker (244)
11. 7
12. Tom ' Pongo' Waring (49)
13. Villa Park
14. 1973
15. The Lamb Ground
16. Dave Stevens

Barnsley FC

1. 1887
2. Barnsley St Peter's
3. Oakwell Stadium
4. Litesome
5. Taits
6. Arthur Fairclough
7. Paul Heckingbottom
8. Angus MacDonald

9. Barry Murphy (569)

10. Ernie Hine (131)

11. 1

12. Cecil McCormack (33)

13. Oakwell

14. 2007

15. Dorothy Hyman Sports Centre

16. Ian Clark

Birmingham City FC

1. 1875

2. Small heath Alliance

3. Bordesley Green

4. Umbro

5. Ansells

6. Alfred Jones

7. Harry Redknapp

8. Paul Robinson

9. Gil Merrick (551)

10. Joe Bradford (267)

11. 2

12. Walter Abbott (34)

13. St Andrews

14. 1968

15. The Autotech Stadium

16. Marc Skinner

Blackburn Rovers FC

1. 1875
2. Oozehead
3. Umbro
4. Perspex
5. Thomas Mitchell
6. Tony Mowbray
7. Charlie Mulgrew
8. Derek Fazackerley (596)
9. Simon Garner (194)
10. 6
11. Ted Harper (43)
12. Ewood Park

13. 1991

14. Irongate

15. Gemma Donnelly

Blackpool FC

1. 1887

2. Preston North End

3. Dole Lane

4. Umbro

5. Easywear

6. Tom Barcroft

7. Gary Bowyer

8. Andy Taylor

9. Jimmy Armfield (569)

10. Jimmy Hampson (252)

11. 1

12. Jimmy Hampson (45)

13. Bloomfield Road

14. 2008

15. Hallgate Park

16. Ryan Lewis

Bolton Wanderers FC

1. 1874
2. Christ Church FC
3. Pike's Lane
4. Bukta
5. Knight Security
6. Tom Rawthorne
7. Phil Parkinson
8. Darren Pratley
9. Eddie Hopkinson (578)
10. Nat Lofthouse (285)
11. 4
12. Joe Smith (38)
13. Macro Stadium

Bradford City AFC

1. 1903
2. Leeds United

3. Valley Parade

4. Patrick

5. National Breakdown
6. Robert Campbell

7. Stuart McCall

8. Romain Vincelot

9. Ces Podd (574)

10. Bobby Campbell (143)

11. 1

12. David Layne (36)

13. Valley Parade

14. 1988

15. Dennyfield

16. Steve Winterburn

Brighton & Hove Albion FC

1. 1901

2. Crystal Palace

3. Goldstone Ground

4. Bukta

5. British Caledonian Airways

6. John Jackson

7. Chris Hughton

8. Bruno

9. Tug Wilson (509)

10. Tommy Cook (114)

11. 1

12. Peter Ward (32)

13. Falmer Stadium

14. 1991

15. Withdean Stadium

16. Hope Powell

Burnley FC

1. 1882

2. Burnley Rovers FC

3. Turf Moor

4. Umbro

5. POCO

6. Harry Bradshaw

7. Sean Dyche
8. Tom Heaton
9. Jerry Dawson (569)
10. George Beel (188)
11. 1
12. George Beel (35)
13. Turf Moor
14. 1995
15. Barden Sports Ground
16. Matt Bee

Cardiff City FC

1. 1899
2. Riversdie AFC
3. Sophia Gardens
4. Umbro
5. Whitbread Wales
6. Davy McDougall
7. Neil Warnock

8. Sean Morrison

9. Billy Hardy (590)

10. Len Davies (179)

11. 1

12. Robert Earnshaw (31)

13. Cardiff City Stadium

14. 1975

15. Cardiff International Sports Stadium

16. Gary Green

Chelsea FC

1. 1905

2. Tottenham

3. Stamford Bridge

4. Umbro

5. Gulf Air

6. John Tait Robertson

7. Antonio Conte

8. Gary Cahill

9. Ron Harris (795)

10. Frank (Lampard (211)

11. 7

12. Jimmy Greaves (43)

13. Stamford Bridge

14. 1992

15. Kingsmeadow

16. Emma Hayes

<u>Charlton Athletic AFC</u>

1. 1905

2. Millwall

3. Siemens Meadow

4. Bukta

5. Fads

6. Walter Rayner

7. Karl Robinson

8. Johnnie Jackson

9. Sam Bartram (623)

10. Derek Hales (168)

11. 1

12. Ralph Allen (33)
13. The Valley
14. 2000
15. Bayliss Avenue
16. Riteesh Mishra

<u>Coventry City FC</u>

1. 1883
2. Singers FC
3. Dowells Field
4. Umbro
5. Talbot Cars
6. William Stanley
7. Mark Robins
8. Michael Doyle
9. Steve Ogrizovic (601)
10. Clarrie Bourton (182)
11. 1
12. Clarrie Bourton (50)
13. Ricoh Arena

14. 1991

15. Coleshill Town FC

16. Jay Bradford

Crystal Palace FC

1. 1905

2. Millwall

3. Crystal Palace

4. Umbro

5. Red Rose

6. Jack Robson

7. Roy Hodgson

8. Jason Puncheon

9. Jim Cannon (660)

10. Peter Simpson (165)

11. 2

12. Peter Simpson (54)

13. Selhurst park

14. 1992

15. Hayles Lane

16. Dean Davenport

Derby County FC

1. 1884
2. Nottingham Forest
3. Racecourse Ground
4. Umbro
5. British Midlands
6. Harry Newbould
7. Gary Rowett
8. Richard Keogh
9. Kevin Hector (589)
10. Steve Bloomer (332)
11. 1
12. Jack Bowers (43)
13. Pride Park Stadium
14. 1989
15. The Don Amott LG Arena
16. John Bennet

Everton FC

1. 1878
2. St Domingo FC
3. Stanley Park
4. Umbro
5. Chang Beer
6. William Edward Barclay
7. Ronald Koeman
8. Phil Jagielka
9. Neville Southall (751)
10. Dixie Dean (383)
11. 5
12. Dixie Dean (60)
13. Goodison Park
14. 1983
15. Select Security Stadium
16. Andy Spence

Fulham FC

1. 1879

2. Fulham St Andrews Church Sunday School FC
3. Hurlingham Park
4. Umbro
5. William Younger
6. Harry bradshaw
7. Slavisa Jokanovic
8. Tom Cairney
9. Jonny Haynes (658)
10. Gordon Davies (178)
11. 1
12. Frank Newton (43)
13. Craven Cottage
14. 1993
15. Middlesex Stadium
16. 2010

Huddersfield Town AFC

1. 1908
2. Leeds United
3. Leeds Road

4. Bukta

5. Central Mirfield

6. Fred Walker

7. David Wagner

8. Tommy Smith

9. Billy Smith (574)

10. George Brown (159)

11. 1

12. Sammy Taylor (42)

13. Kirklees Stadium

14. 1988

15. Storthes Hall

16. Ashley Vickers

Hull City FC

1. 1904

2. Leeds United

3. The Boulevard

4. Europa

5. Hygena

6. James Ramster

7. Leonid Slutsky

8. Michael Dawson

9. Andy Davidson (579)

10. Chris Chilton (222)

11. 1

12. Stuart Elliott (27)

13. KCOM Stadium

14. 2001

15. Hull University

16. Rachel Gay

Ipswich Town FC

1. 1878

2. Ipswich AFC

3. Broom Hill

4. Mick O'Brien

5. Mick McCarthy

6.

7. Luke Chambers

8. Mick Mills (737)

9. Ray Crawford (218)

10. 1

11. Ted Phillips (46)

12. Portman Road

13. The Goldstar Ground

14. Ralph Pruden

Leeds United FC

1. 1919

2. Manchester United

3. Elland Road

4. Umbro

5. RFW

6. Dick Ray

7. Thomas Christiansen

8. Liam Cooper

9. Jack Charlton (773)

10. Peter Lorimer (238)
11. 1

12. John Charles (42)
13. Ellan Road
14. 1989
15. Garforth Town AFC
16. Bob Wilkinson

Leicester City FC

1. 1884
2. Leicester Fosse FC
3. Fosse Road
4. Bukta
5. Ind Coope
6. Ernest Marson
7. Craig Shakespeare
8. Wes Morgan
9. Graham Cross (599)
10. Arthur Chandler (273)
11. 4
12. Arthur Rowley (44)
13.

14. King Power Stadium
15. 2004
16. Riverside Pavilion
17. Jonathan Morgan

Liverpool FC

1. 1892
2. Manchester united
3. Anfield
4. Umbro
5. Hitachi
6. William Edward Barclay
7. Jurgen Klopp
8. Jordan Henderson
9. Ian Callaghan (857)
10. Ian Rush (346)
11. 7
12. Ian Rush (47)
13. Anfield
14. 1989

15. Select Security Stadium

16. Scott Rogers

Manchester City FC

1. 1880

2. St Mark's (West Gorton)

3. West Gorton

4. Umbro

5. SAAB

6. Frederick Hopkinson

7. Pep Guardiola

8. Vincent Kompany

9. Alan Oakes (676)

10. Eric Brook (177)

11. 5

12. Tommy Johnson (38)

13. City of Manchester Stadium

14. 1988

15. Academy Stadium

16. Nick Cushing

Manchester United FC

1. 1878
2. Newton Heath LYR FC
3. North Road
4. Umbro
5. Sharp Electronics
6. A.H. Albut
7. Jose Mourinho
8. Michael Carrick
9. Ryan Giggs (963)
10. Wayne Rooney (253)
11. 12
12. Dennis Law (46)
13. Old Trafford

Middlesborough FC

1. 1876
2. Sunderland
3. Albert Park
4. Bukta

5. Datsun Cleveland
6. Jack Robson
7. Garry Monk
8. Grant Leadbitter
9. Tim Williamson (602)
10. Gerorge Camsell (345)
11. 1
12. George Camsell (63)
13. Riverside Stadium
14. 1978
15. Teesdale Park
16. Lindsey Stephenson

Newcastle United FC

1. 1892
2. Sunderland
3. St James' Park
4. Bukta
5. Fun 88
6. Frank Watt

7. Rafael Benitez
8. Jamaal Lascelles
9. Jimmy Lawrence (496)
10. Alan Shearer (206)
11. 6
12. Andy Cole (41)
13. St James's Park
14. 1989
15. Craik Park
16. Andy Innes

Norwich City FC

1. 1902
2. Ipswich Town
3. Newmarket Road
4. Umbro
5. Poll Withey Windows
6. John Bowman
7. Daniel Farke
8. Russell Martin

9. Kevin Keelan (673)

10. Johnny Gavin (122)

11. Ralph Hunt (31)

12. Carrow Road

13. 1991

14. Plantation Park

15. Mel Swift

Nottingham Forest FC

1. 1865

2. Nottingham Forest Football & Bandy Club

3. Forest Recreation Ground

4. Umbro

5. Panasonic

6. Harry Radford

7. Mark Warburton

8. Chris Cohen

9. Bob Mckinlay (692)

10. Grenville Morris (217)

11. 2

12. Wally Ardron (36)

13. City Ground

14. 1990

15. Basford United FC

16. Graham Abercrombie

Oldham Athletic FC

1. 1895

2. Pine Villa FC

3. Atletic Ground

4. Umbro

5. David Ashworth

6. John Sheridan

7. Peter Clarke

8. Ian Wood (582)

9. Roger Palmer (156)

10. 3

11. Tom Davis (33)

12. Boundary Park

Portsmouth FC

1. 1898
2. Southampton
3. Fratton Park
4. Umbro
5. Fiat
6. Frank Bretell
7. Kenny Jackett
8. Brett Pitman
9. Jimmy Dickinson (834)
10. Peter Harris (194)
11. 2
12. Guy Whittingham (42)
13. Fratton Park
14. 1987
15. Privett Park
16. Jay Sadler

Queens Park Rangers FC

1. 1882

2. St Jude's
3. Queens Park
4. Admiral
5. Guinness
6. James Cowan
7. Ian Holloway
8. Nedum Onuoha
9. Tony Ingham (548)
10. George Goddard (186)
11. 1
12. Rodney Marsh (44)
13. Loftus Road Stadium
14. 2001
15. Honeycroft
16. Martino Chevannes

Reading FC

1. 1871
2. Aldershot Town
3. Reading Recreation Ground

4. Umbro
5. Reading Chronicle
6. Joseph Edward Sydenham
7. Jaap Stam
8. Paul McShane
9. Martin Hicks (603)
10. Trevor Senior (191)
11. 2
12. Ronnie Blackman (39)
13. Madejski Stadium
14. 2006
15. Adams Park
16. Kelly Chambers

Sheffield United FC

1. 1889
2. Sheffield Wednesday
3. Bramall Lane
4. Umbro
5. Cantor's

6. J.B. Wostinholm

7. Chris Wilder

8. Billy Sharp

9. Joe Shaw (631)

10. Harry Johnson (201)

11. 4

12. Jimmy Dunne (41)

13. Bramall Lane

14. 1998

15. Handsworth WMC

16. Dan O'Hearne

Sheffield Wednesday FC

1. 1867

2. Sheffield united

3. HighField

4. Umbro

5. Arthur Dickinson

6. Carlos Carvalhal

7. Glen Loovens

8. Andrew Wilson (560)

9. Andrew Wilson (217)

10. 3

11. Derek Dooley (46)

12. Hillsborough

13. 1971

14. Sheffield Hallam University Sports Park

15. Dave Higgins

<u>Southampton FC</u>

1. 1885

2. St Mary's Y.M.A.

3. The Common

4. Umbro

5. Rank Xerox

6. Cecil Knight

7. Mauricio Pellegrino

8. Stephen Davis

9. Terry Paine (815)

10. Mick Channon (228)

11. 1

12. Derek Reeves (44)

13. St Mary's Stadium

14. 1979

15. Silverlake Arena

16. Adam Lee

Stoke City FC

1. 1863

2. Stoke Ramblers

3. Lonsdale Street

4. Admiral

5. Ricoh

6. Thomas Slaney

7. Mark Hughes

8. Ryan Shawcross

9. Eric Skeels (597)

10. John Ritchie (176)

11. 1

12. Charlie Wilson & Arthur Griffiths (38)

13. Bet365 Stadium

14. 2001

15. Community Drive

16. Steve Swanwick

Sunderland AFC

1. 1879

2. Sunderland & District Teachers AFC

3. Blue House Field

4. Umbro

5. Cowie's

6. Tom Watson

7. Simon Grayson

8. Lee Cattermole

9. Jimmy Montgomery (627)

10. Bobby Gurney (228)

11. 2

12. Dave Halliday (43)

13. Stadium of Light

14. 1989

15. Mariners Park

16. Melanie Reay

Swansea City AFC

1. 1912

2. Swansea Town AFC

3. Vetch Field

4. Bukta

5. Diversified Products

6. Walter Whittaker

7. Paul Clement

8. Leon Britton

9. Wilfred Milne (586)

10. Ivor Allchurch (166)

11. 2

12. Cyril Pearce (35)

13. Liberty Stadium

14. 2002

15. Llandarcy Academy of Sport

16. Ian Owen

Swindon Town FC

1. 1879
2. Swindon AFC
3. Bradford Road
4. Umbro
5. ISIS
6. Sam Allen
7. David Flitcroft
8. Olly Lancashire
9. John Trollope (889)
10. Harry Morris (229)
11. 2
12. Harry Morris (48)
13. County Ground
14. 1993
15. Barrington Park
16. Leonie Wade

Tottenham Hotspur FC

1. 1882

2. Hotspur FC
3. Tottenham marshes
4. Umbro
5. Holsten
6. Frank Brettell
7. Mauricio Pochettino
8. Hugo Lloris
9. Steve Perryman (854)
10. Jimmy Greaves (266)
11. 8
12. Clive Allen (49)
13. Wembley Stadium
14. 1985
15. Chesthunt Stadium
16. Karen Hills

Watford FC

1. 1881
2. Watford Rovers
3. Cassiobury Park

4. Umbro

5. Iveco

6. John Goddall

7. Marco Silva

8. Troy Deeney

9. Luther Blissett (503)

10. Luther Blissett (186)

11. 1

12. Cliff Holton (48)

13. Vicarage Road

14. 1970

15. Kings Langley FC

16. Keith Boanas

West Bromwih Albion FC

1. 1878

2. West Bromwich Strollers

3. Coopers Hill

4. Diadora

5. BSR Housewares

6. Louis Ford
7. Tony Pulis
8. Jonny Evans
9. Tony Brown (720)
10. Tony Brown (279)
11. W.G. Richardson (40)
12. 5
13. The hawthorns
14. 1989
15. Dales Lane, Rushall
16. Louis Sowe

West Ham United FC

1. 1895
2. Thames Ironworks
3. Hermit Road
4. Admiral
5. AVCO Trust
6. Syd King
7. Slaven Bilic

8. Mark Noble
9. Billy Bonds (799)
10. Vic Watson (326)
11. 3
12. Vic Watson (50)
13. London Stadium
14. 1991
15. London Community Track
16. Greg de Carnys

Wigan Athletic FC

1. 1932
2. Bolton Wanderers
3. Springfield Park
4. Umbro
5. Charlie Spencer
6. Paul Cook
7. Sam Morsy
8. Kevin Langley (317)
9. Andy Liddell (70)

10. 1

11. Graeme Jones (31)

12. DW Stadium

Wimbledon

1. 1889
2. Wimbledon Old Central FC
3. Wimbledon Common
4. Bukta
5. Golddigger
6. H.R. Watts
7. Robbie Neilson
8. Dean Lewington
9. Roy Law (644)
10. Eddie Reynolds (340)
11. 1
12. Alan Cork (29)
13. National Hockey Stadium

Wolverhampton Wanderers FC

1. 1877
2. St. Luke's
3. Goldthorn Hill
4. Umbro
5. George Worrall
6. Nuni Espirito Santo
7. Daniel Batth
8. Derek Parkin (609)
9. Steve Bull (306)
10. 4
11. Steve Bull (52)
12. Molineux Stadium
13. 1975
14. Keys Park, Hednesford
15. Tim Dudding

21627187R00082

Printed in Poland
by Amazon Fulfillment
Poland Sp. z o.o., Wrocław